HORSEPOWER

INDY CARS

by Carrie A. Braulick

Reading Consultant:
Barbara J. Fox
Reading Specialist
North Carolina State University

Capstone press

Mankato, Minnesota

Blazers is published by Capstone Press,
151 Good Counsel Drive, P.O. Box 669, Mankato, Minnesota 56002.
www.capstonepress.com

Library of Congress Cataloging-in-Publication Data
Braulick, Carrie A., 1975–
    Indy cars / by Carrie A. Braulick.
    p. cm.—(Blazers. Horsepower)
    Summary: "Describes Indy race cars, including their design,
engines, tires, and safety features"—Provided by publisher.
    Includes bibliographical references and index.
    ISBN 0-7368-4390-6 (hardcover)
    ISBN 0-7368-6171-8 (softcover)
    1. Indy cars—Juvenile literature. I. Title. II. Series.
TL236.B73 2006
629.228—dc22   2004028831

Credits
Jason Knudson, set designer; Patrick D. Dentinger, book
    designer; Kelly Garvin, photo researcher; Scott Thoms,
    photo editor

Photo Credits
Artemis Images/Earl Ma, 7, 12, 13, 18, 19, 22–23, 25, 26, 27
Corbis/Michael Kim, 8 (left), 9 (right), 14; Reuters, 20, 21;
    Reuters/Robin Jerstad, 11; William Manning, 17
Getty Images, Inc./Gavin Lawrence, cover; Jamie Squire, 5;
    Jonathan Ferrey, 8–9, 28–29; Robert Laberge, 6

**Capstone Press thanks Betty Carlan, Research Librarian at the International
Motorsports Hall of Fame in Talladega, Alabama, for her assistance in preparing
this book.**

1 2 3 4 5 6 10 09 08 07 06 05

TABLE OF CONTENTS

INDY CARS

Indy cars line up behind the starting line. The flagman waves a green flag. The Indy cars roar down the racetrack.

Car number 10 takes the lead. Later, another car bumps it from behind. The number 10 car spins out and crashes.

BLAZER FACT

In early Indy car races, both a driver and a mechanic rode in a car. The mechanic made car repairs right on the track.

The driver of the yellow number 4 car speeds away from a pit stop. He passes the wrecked car. Soon, he takes the lead and wins the race.

POWER AND SPEED

Indy cars race at tracks throughout North America. The cars are named after the famous Indy 500 race.

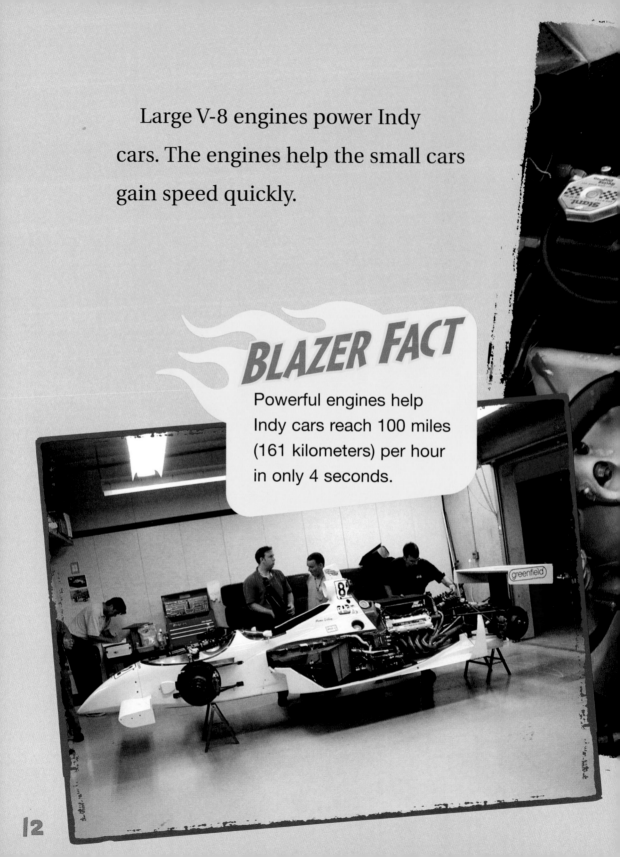

Large V-8 engines power Indy cars. The engines help the small cars gain speed quickly.

BLAZER FACT

Powerful engines help Indy cars reach 100 miles (161 kilometers) per hour in only 4 seconds.

Rear wing

visit iShares.com

Front wing

Indy cars have front and rear wings. The wings push air down on the cars. They help the cars grip the track.

Built for Racing

Early Indy cars were shaped
like boxes. Modern Indy cars are
shaped like bullets. This shape
helps the cars travel quickly.

Indy cars have smooth tires called slicks. The tires wear down during races. Pit crews may replace a car's tires 10 times in one race.

A pit crew can change all four of an Indy car's tires and fill its gas tank in only 16 seconds.

Indy cars have safety features to protect drivers. Tires are designed to fall off during a crash. Without tires, a wrecked car slides instead of rolling.

The Indy 500 track has a soft wall. The wall absorbs the shock of a car hitting it.

INDY CAR DIAGRAM

Fuel port

Boost limiter

Rear wing

Air deflector

Front wing

Tire

Indy Cars in Action

Most races are on large oval-shaped tracks. Other races are on street courses through cities.

Street course

Drivers depend on their cars and their teams. Even the best drivers need help from others to win races.

HEADING INTO A TURN!

GLOSSARY

bullet (BUL-it)—a small, pointed metal object fired from a gun

flagman (FLAYG-man)—the person who waves the flags that signal race car drivers to go, stop, or travel slowly

mechanic (muh-KAN-ik)—someone who fixes vehicles or machinery

pit stop (PIT STOP)—a stop that a driver makes during a race to change tires or get fuel

slick (SLIK)—a smooth tire used to race on paved surfaces

street course (STREET KORSS)—an Indy car race held on city streets

wing (WING)—a long, flat panel on the front or back of an Indy car

READ MORE

Bledsoe, Glen, and Karen Bledsoe. *The World's Fastest Indy Cars.* Built for Speed. Mankato, Minn.: Capstone Press, 2003.

Fish, Bruce, and Becky Durost Fish. *Indy Car Racing.* Race Car Legends. Philadelphia: Chelsea House, 2001.

Sessler, Peter C., and Nilda Sessler. *Indy Cars.* Off to the Races. Vero Beach, Fla.: Rourke, 1999.

INTERNET SITES

FactHound offers a safe, fun way to find Internet sites related to this book. All of the sites on FactHound have been researched by our staff.

Here's how:

1. Visit *www.facthound.com*
2. Type in this special code **0736843906** for age-appropriate sites. Or, enter a search word related to this book for a more general search.
3. Click on the **Fetch It** button.

FactHound will fetch the best sites for you!

INDEX